This book differs from traditional management books. It doesn't deal only with the techniques of management—goal setting, time management, meeting objectives. Instead, it focuses on developing a positive attitude to carry with you into your work setting, an attitude that stems naturally from your balance of the professional, personal, and spiritual aspects of your life. For once you accept the fact that you are a multidimensional human being, you'll be able to better understand your own behavior and cope more easily with everyday management decisions.

THE THOUGHT-A-WEEK GUIDES: HOW TO BE A BETTER MANAGER

A Blue Cliff Editions Book

Gloria Lanza-Bajo

BALLANTINE BOOKS • NEW YORK

ACKNOWLEDGMENTS

I thank my husband Ted and daughter Christine for their patience as I developed these thoughts. I especially thank the Pathwork lectures for teaching me to be responsible for my own happiness and well-being, both at home and in the workplace. Finally, I thank Jason Shulman for giving me the opportunity to write this book and my editor, Melinda Corey, for what she did to make my messages clearer.

Library of Congress Catalog Card Number: 86-91661

ISBN 0-345-33344-6

Printed in Canada

First Edition: June 1987

CONTENTS

Introduction

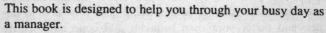

This book is designed to help you through your busy day as a manager.

The title of manager can be applied to a wide variety of jobs. You may be a top-level executive at a major corporation with a large staff or an office manager in a small company. The depth of responsibilities from one job to another may differ radically, but the duties remain the same: organizing and setting priorities and accomplishing short- and long-term goals. And no matter what kind of manager you are, you face the same basic challenges in the workplace: getting along with your staff, making sure they complete their responsibilities on time, nurturing them to meet their potential.

As a manager, you also have a number of responsibilities to yourself. The most important of these is maintaining the balance in your three separate lives—your professional, personal, and spiritual lives. Your professional self is your life as a manager. It is concerned with your job and your career activities. Your personal self deals with your relationships with others—your spouse, your parents, your friends, your children. Your spiritual self searches to be at peace in the world and to find a larger meaning in your life. The spiritual self is the essence of who you really are—and what you bring as an individual to the professional and personal aspects of your life. This book will show you how to incorporate all aspects of yourself into your role as a manager.

The Thought-a-Week Guide: How to Be a Better Manager differs from traditional management books. It doesn't deal only with the techniques of management—goal setting, time management, meeting objectives. Instead, it focuses on developing a positive attitude to carry with you into your work setting, an attitude that stems naturally from your balance of the professional, personal, and spiritual aspects of your life. For once you accept the fact that you are a multidimensional human being, you'll be able to understand better your own behavior and cope more easily with everyday management decisions.

There are a number of ways you can use this book. For example, you may want to open it at random, search for a thought that applies to a situation that concerns you, and use the ideas to help you solve your problem. Or you may choose to use this book as a course of study, starting at the beginning and going through each of the fifty-two thoughts consecutively. Whatever way you choose, by the end of the year, you will have developed new techniques that may make you a more efficient manager as well as new ways of thinking that may heighten your sense of inner peace and help achieve harmony in your life. I offer this book with these hopes in mind.

Think positive.

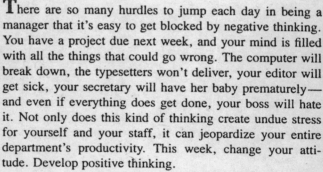

There are so many hurdles to jump each day in being a manager that it's easy to get blocked by negative thinking. You have a project due next week, and your mind is filled with all the things that could go wrong. The computer will break down, the typesetters won't deliver, your editor will get sick, your secretary will have her baby prematurely—and even if everything does get done, your boss will hate it. Not only does this kind of thinking create undue stress for yourself and your staff, it can jeopardize your entire department's productivity. This week, change your attitude. Develop positive thinking.

Here is how it works. You are facing a stressful situation—for instance, you have completed an important marketing plan, and you present it to top management. Rather than attempting to anticipate their reactions, evaluate your performance and put your mind at rest. Ask yourself these questions: Did I do my best in preparing the plan? Did I do a thorough job? Am I confident enough about it to take responsibility for it? If you can answer yes to these questions, you can feel calm and self-assured. You can assume that your interactions with your superiors will be successful, because you have already given your best and can expect only good from your efforts.

3

A positive attitude can also help to defuse potentially volatile situations. If you find a certain project is going to be difficult, accept its stumbling blocks as opportunities to learn and grow as a manager. Or if your staff is feeling overwhelmed with work, give them your encouragement. Let them know that you believe they can do the job.

Your positive attitude will make your work move more steadily, and may even make the office more efficient. After all, positive thinking is infectious.

Concentration is the cornerstone of efficiency.

In the middle of a hectic day, you may suddenly find yourself wandering from one task to another aimlessly, without accomplishing anything. It is easy to become overwhelmed when there seems to be too much to do and far too little time to do it in. But instead of trying to react to the whirlwind around you, stop for a minute. Take a deep breath and focus on the job at hand. This is concentration —focusing on one event or action at a time and giving it your full attention.

To be a good manager, you need to be able to accomplish your objectives and meet your deadlines, and the only way to see results is to concentrate and work on one thing at a time. For example, that means completing the quarterly budget projection *before* you start on the summary of last week's convention and only *after* you have prepared your speech for your big presentation next month. Don't worry about one thing while doing another.

This week, commit yourself to focusing on one activity at a time. When you feel distracted, stop, take a deep breath, and count to twenty-five. Then return to your work. Repeat this exercise as often as you want throughout the day. You'll find that your concentration and your energy level will improve; so will your efficiency as a manager.

Frustration is a natural part of management.

When you decided to become a manager, you unconsciously said yes to coping with frustration. Many managers forget how frustrating the daily routine can be. Yet many of the things that cause the frustration are themselves part of the job—long meetings, minor daily crises, impromptu conferences with your staff. These interruptions force you to postpone seemingly more important tasks, which just seems to get in the way for a manager concerned with deadlines and results. This week, we'll learn how to handle this natural frustration.

Your first step toward coping with frustration is to accept it. Understand that *all* your day's activities are inherently important—even the ones you do not like—because they are all part of your job. If you find that your greatest problem lies in completing routine tasks, set aside a specific time each day to work on them. An hour of concentrated effort at the beginning or end of the day could take care of those bothersome duties. To ensure that you give your staff enough attention but that they don't monopolize your day, schedule a regular meeting time rather than letting them pass through your office at any time. If you need time to yourself, close your door for an hour or so.

This week, accept even your routine tasks as an integral

part of your management life, and organize your schedule so that you can deal with them quickly and effectively. That will allow you to keep the natural frustration of being a manager from becoming an overwhelming burden, and will free you to experience the greater rewards of your job.

Be respected; don't worry about being liked.

The business of being a manager is making difficult choices. As a manager, you are always making decisions for the good of the project, your department, or the company—some of which may not make you popular with colleagues or individuals on your staff. These decisions can range from the relatively simple—asking your staff to work late, choosing to promote a colleague—to the very difficult—firing a staff member, being forced to cut back. Whether large or small, these situations are always problematic, particularly when you are sensitive to people's feelings and are aware that your decisions may be difficult for some to accept. But these troublesome decisions become unbearable chores when you are worried about being liked.

Nearly everyone wants to win approval from the people around them. But trying to please everyone is a deadly trap, a no-win situation. You can't please everyone all the time—and you shouldn't try, especially when you are a manager who must balance the needs of a staff with a company's objectives.

This week, examine what you avoid dealing with because you worry you will not be liked. Do you find that you delay difficult decisions because you are afraid of what your staff or colleagues will think? Remember that it is your *job* to make the right decision. Realize that if you make the right choice for the company and the task at hand, you will gain the respect of those around you. Most people accept a good decision once they understand it. Part of gaining respect from others is helping them understand how you have made your decision. You will be admired for your willingness to do what is right, even if it makes you unpopular in some circles.

This week, accept the fact that as a manager, you will not always be liked. Strive instead to be respected.

Accept that you will not always be right.

Being a manager means that you may be wrong from time to time. When you claim your authority and take a stand, you cannot always predict the outcome. And when things don't turn out the way you planned, you have to change your course so that they run smoothly again.

But when you spend your time worrying about being right, you sap your power and become paralyzed. If you hesitate because you don't want to be "wrong" or fear ruining a "perfect" image, you render yourself unable to act, which inevitably has serious effects on your job performance. Your worry leads you to procrastinate about making decisions, to avoid discussions with top management, to wallow in the status quo when you need to be innovative.

This week, accept the fact that as a manager and a human being, you will make mistakes. Realize, too, that in most cases, you are the only one who feels you have to remain perfect. No one else is keeping track. What's more, most people know that mistakes are part and parcel of being in the business world. What distinguishes the true leader isn't the way she avoids problems, but the way she deals with them. A true leader accepts the responsibility and frustration of being wrong and uses her mistakes as a stepping-stone to a greater understanding of herself and her business. For example, in your haste to rush a project through, you may push your staff so hard that their morale starts to suffer, and instead of getting the job done, they grind to a halt. At this point, you need to acknowledge that you have been wrong and move to create a new schedule that will accommodate both your employees' needs and your boss's deadline. This approach means taking risks. It means being a leader.

This week, decide to become a leader. Accept that you will not always be right. Say yes to risks.

Manage your time.

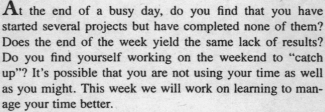

At the end of a busy day, do you find that you have started several projects but have completed none of them? Does the end of the week yield the same lack of results? Do you find yourself working on the weekend to "catch up"? It's possible that you are not using your time as well as you might. This week we will work on learning to manage your time better.

The first step is knowing how you use your time. For the beginning of the week, set up a log and record what you do during the workday. Divide your log into half-hour segments and be precise in entering the time you spend on a given project or activity. After a couple of days, examine the log as a whole. Notice how often you are on the phone, when you do most of your writing, how often you handle employee problems, how much time you spend at meetings.

After you have reviewed your log thoroughly, decide where you can make changes to become more efficient. Are there activities you should delegate to your staff? Are all your tasks necessary? What would happen if something wasn't done?

After you form a picture of your work schedule, reorganize your time. If you are doing tasks that don't make good use of your time, delegate some of them to others. If you are more creative in the morning, use that time to do your most challenging work. Finally, eliminate the tasks that simply waste everyone's time.

This week, examine your schedule and change your habits. You will work more efficiently and you will feel better about your performance on the job.

Be in the now.

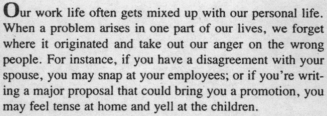

Our work life often gets mixed up with our personal life. When a problem arises in one part of our lives, we forget where it originated and take out our anger on the wrong people. For instance, if you have a disagreement with your spouse, you may snap at your employees; or if you're writing a major proposal that could bring you a promotion, you may feel tense at home and yell at the children.

If you find yourself lashing out at people more frequently and you can't figure out why, you need to look beyond the symptoms of your dissatisfaction. Look at the totality of your life. Examine all your different lives—your home life, your work life, your spiritual life. In so doing, you may find that you need to learn to separate these lives. You need to be and act in the now.

This week, learn to live in the now. Experience life as it is happening. If you are at work, live by its expectations, by its way of thinking, with its people. Do the same for your life at home and for your spiritual life.

Now examine whether you are unconsciously transferring tension from one part of your life to another, unconsciously allowing a situation in one to affect your attitude in another. Are you letting your goals in one part of your life affect your other lives? Are you so busy rushing through your work life to get to the top that you have lost sight of where you are right now with your family, your friends, and yourself? Understanding these conflicts will help you to cope with each area of your life separately and appropriately.

You will find that the now is the most fulfilling place to be. It is the only place you can effect changes in all of your lives and truly enjoy what you are doing.

Be patient with yourself.

Because our lives are so complicated, we cannot devote ourselves to every part of it as completely as we might like. We can't do everything perfectly; there isn't enough time. This week, accept these limitations and be more patient with yourself.

For example, you may have a tight deadline on an important project at work. In the midst of working on it, you may also be planning major renovations to your house and packing your first child off to college. Your schedule seems overwhelming, and even small things try your patience. Perhaps more upsetting is that you feel as if you are cheating yourself and others because you feel you cannot give your best at work or at home.

This week, determine whether you are being unnecessarily impatient with yourself. Draw up a list of the priorities in your various lives—your business life, your personal life, your spiritual life. Now, determine how much time and effort these priorities take in your lives. Then assess realistically how much time you can devote to them. Keep a log if you feel it will be helpful. Next, with this information in mind, plan changes. You may find that you need to adjust your work schedule—maybe begin work earlier in the day so you can spend more time with your family, or set project schedules that will not keep you in the office over the weekends. Or you may find that you need to change your personal life—maybe cut down on some current activities for the moment or postpone travel plans.

Whatever you do, once you establish a clearer focus for your life, you will work more efficiently and enjoy yourself more fully. Your managerial skills will serve you better if you are patient with yourself and with the time it takes to get things done.

Listen for the message.

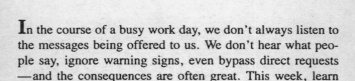

In the course of a busy work day, we don't always listen to the messages being offered to us. We don't hear what people say, ignore warning signs, even bypass direct requests —and the consequences are often great. This week, learn to listen for the message.

Sometimes messages around your office may be direct and simple to handle. An employee who's been having a family emergency needs to have you assign someone else to complete his project. If you are sensitive to his direct message for help, you'll serve him well, and your department won't be left stranded. Just set aside the time to listen to him. Other messages are more indirect. More often than not, they're the result of office chatter. Remember to keep your ears open—your staff usually know more than you do about the tensions within a department. They can detect a potentially disruptive feud or hint at problems with meeting deadlines; you can listen and take action on them. The most troublesome problems may stem from your own rigidity. You may have become so fixed about how the office is run that you cannot accept alternative solutions. For example, if a new computer system has been installed in your office, and you don't have time to learn it, but two of your staff members offer to train people, accept their offer. Instead of worrying that you are relinquishing your power, spend your time planning and taking care of the managerial duties that make better use of your time.

True leaders are able to assimilate everything going on around them and come to intelligent solutions. This week, examine how often you do not hear what people are really saying. Vow to listen for the messages that need to be heard, both direct and indirect—and watch the communication and the efficiency improve greatly.

Develop your people.

Do you know how to nurture your employees' talents? Constantly developing skills and talents is essential to maintaining a well-informed, satisfied staff as well as a respected, forward-looking company. It isn't enough just to oversee people: You must know who your people are and how to guide them to use their fullest potential. This week, examine how well you develop your people, and consider ways to improve your techniques.

To nurture your employees, you need to take a multi-level approach that includes both formal and informal methods of nurturing growth: a specific appraisal program, access to professional development programs, and, most important, a commitment to help them grow personally and professionally.

Regular meetings with your staff are an ideal time to formally challenge them to improve their performance. You can set incentives, offer bonuses, or encourage them to set stronger goals for themselves. Do some of your employees have particular needs? Do they need to improve their writing skills? Are their work techniques effective? Offer them opportunities to take courses or seminars that will help them meet their goals. If your company provides reimbursement for courses, let them know about it.

This points up how important it is for you to be familiar with your company's policies for professional and personal development. Be sure they are written clearly and administered fairly. Speak with your personnel manager and other managers in various departments to form a complete picture of what your company does to hang on to its employees. Then make sure all your employees are aware that these policies exist.

Now, plan for the future. Think about how you want your department to develop. In what ways can your employees help your department to grow? Analyze your department carefully to pinpoint people who have potential; then think of ways they might develop and stay with your company. If your company's development programs are inadequate for your department, draw up a list of suggestions and present them to your superiors or your personnel director.

As a manager with direct responsibilities to both individuals and long-term company goals, it is your job to make sure that individual growth and company growth go hand in hand. Your rewards are great: more inspired, more creative employees and a more progressive workplace.

Be supportive, not critical.

Employees may not always measure up to our standards of good performance. Yet when you are displeased with them, you always have a choice of how you respond—either with criticism or support. You will achieve far better results if you choose support rather than criticism.

Being supportive means doing your best to understand your employees' shortcomings and finding ways to reinforce their strengths. Being supportive requires sensitivity and patience on your part as you help people overcome their job-related faults and shortsightedness. It means not simply reacting, but taking the time to listen to your employees' explanations for their mistakes. Doing this will give you the information you need to understand why they are making errors.

When you treat your employees with this kind of supportive attention, you will be more likely to inspire them to do better. By providing a safe environment for them to grow and learn, you encourage them to ask for support before things go too far astray. If, on the other hand, you beat them down with criticism, you only foster fear and resentment. You create tension, which eventually will stifle their productivity and creativity.

Being critical may give you an outlet for your frustra-

tions and impatience, but it does little else. It's taking the
easy way out. It may take less time to say, "You'll never
measure up," but that doesn't get at the root of the problem.

Remember, in taking a supportive stance, you are not
abandoning your critical faculties in evaluating your employees. You're simply manifesting them in a more productive manner. This week, notice how you react to your
employees' mistakes. Take stock of yourself and your employees. Stretch your patience; take time to sit down with
your people and hear what they have to say. Become supportive.

Maintain a sense of humor and reduce the melodrama.

How do you react to events at work? When a minor crisis flares up, do you panic? Do you worry? Do you see these misadventures as part of the never-ending melodrama of your life? You may be taking yourself too seriously. This week, try applying some humor and lightness to regain your perspective.

Humor is an essential ingredient in life and can be a terrific lifesaver on the job. It undercuts the intensity and pretentiousness of any situation. Let's say you are in a seemingly serious situation—an important meeting where you believe everyone present is better than you. At this point, it may be difficult to remember that they are all human beings with hearts, minds, and an array of insecurities. So think of something amusing or absurd that will dispel your anxiety and make you smile. Imagine everyone at the meeting as zoo animals. The chairman is a gorilla, the financial analyst a zebra, the marketing manager a walrus. These images balance your perception of reality and provide you with the equanimity you need. When you are taking *yourself* too seriously, find a mirror and make faces at yourself. Frown, groan, shake your fists, stick your tongue out, even emit a primal scream—anything to break the intensity.

This week, integrate humor into your life in whatever small ways you can. Poke fun at yourself; make quiet jokes in the conference room to relieve tension. Shift the gears in yourself to help you and other people see another way of viewing the world. Humor will turn the raging, melodramatic sea of your life into a quiet, peaceful stream.

Managers are human, too.

Myths about managers run rampant, and most of them are negative. They center on the idea that managers are cold, impersonal decision-makers who want only to get the work done. They don't understand, much less intuit, what their employees need. In fact, they have probably trained themselves to be removed from their own and others' feelings. Do you believe these myths reflect your image or the image you feel you have to maintain? Or are you aware of your humanity?

Being human means that you *do* have reactions to the world around you, that you can't always predict how you'll feel, and that you aren't always in control of your feelings. It means that you understand the strong overlap that must exist between your three lives—your professional, personal, and spiritual selves. You realize that you will always be merging your objective, rational professional self with the personal self and the inner drives of your spiritual self. This knowledge about your humanity increases your depth of understanding and adds a much needed dimension to your management techniques. It gives you perspective and shows others you can be imperfect, even vulnerable. Understanding your humanity allows you to acknowledge it and accept it in your staff.

This week, work on developing your human qualities and appreciating them in others.

First, observe how you interact with the people in your company. Notice how your staff reacts to you. Do they avoid talking to you? Are they defensive? Anxious? Maybe they think you will not accept their errors or shortcomings. Now, think about your past experiences with bosses. What kind of boss did you have—or would have liked to have —when you were learning the ropes and made your first big mistake? Is this the kind of boss you are now? How can you change to become more open to your staff's human foibles and needs? How can you demonstrate your humanity?

This week, rediscover your humanity. Once you do, you will be able to discover it in your staff, too. It will be a revelation to get to know yourself and them.

Don't misuse your power.

□

For a manager, authority means a willingness to take risks, to be responsible, even when you aren't sure of the answers. If your division performs well, you are responsible for doing a good job. If it does not perform well, you are responsible for that, too. You are the final authority. You have to make the decisions. But you must be careful not to misuse this power.

One way people abuse their authority is to leave their employees in the dark. For example, you may tell people what to do but not explain the situation or the rationale behind your decision. This turns what should be a natural flow of information into a nasty power struggle. It makes you look like a dictator, and it engenders a sense of anger and alienation in your workers. Eventually, it may even bring recalcitrance or rebellion. People don't want to be part of a team unless they feel they're playing an active part, with some control over how the game is being played. You can avoid this situation if you simply let your employees know what's going on, even if you can't go into as much detail as they would like.

You can also keep your employees informed by involving them in as many areas of your work as possible. Plan meetings with your staff, set goals together, use teamwork to get the job done. You can remain the clear leader, but you don't have to abuse people by dictating to them and rendering them impotent.

This week, work toward using your power in positive ways. Lead them and keep them involved. Be open to their participation. Do not let them stay in the dark. This will allow you to develop a full, mature authority.

Make your day your own.

Having to react to everyone around you rather than making active choices about your day can be very frustrating. You go to work with the best of intentions. Today is the day you will get your budget finished and plan the work for next quarter. But from the moment you walk into your office, you have a stream of people coming to see you. You respond to them all, helping *them* get *their* work done. Six o'clock comes around, and you find you have met none of your goals. The time has come to take more control of your workday. You need to make your day your own.

Begin by analyzing your responsibilities. Perhaps there are too many people reporting to you—too many people with too few responsibilities. Reorganizing your department and spreading the work load can help. If possible, have one of your staff members act as a liaison for you. Give that person the authority to decide upon minor problems that don't need your attention. It will allow you to put your time to better use.

Now examine your work habits. Maybe they need to change. Set up a daily schedule for getting your work done—and stick to it. Close your door for an hour during the day to concentrate on your paperwork. With this schedule, you will still be available and accessible, but you will also be more disciplined. You will stop reacting solely to everyone else's needs and will focus on your own.

This week, take more control of what is happening in your work environment. You'll feel better about yourself, and the difference in your accomplishments will be astounding.

Be realistic about your weaknesses.

Yes, it's true you're not perfect. You've admitted it to yourself; yet you still think you have to spend half your working day convincing people that you are. In reality, your attempt to appear perfect exhausts you and saps energy you could be devoting to actually doing your job. You will serve yourself and your staff better if you are realistic about admitting your weaknesses and try to find ways to minimize their effects in your workplace.

Let's begin by taking a personal inventory of your weaknesses. Are you a poor administrator but a great idea person? Or are you a strong leader but a procrastinator? Are you afraid to put things in writing because you don't want to be responsible for what you've said? Do you encourage your staff to come up with new ideas but find fault with everything they say? Be honest. Solving problems is impossible unless you admit them first.

After you've taken stock of your problem areas, begin to accept responsibility for improving them. In many cases, that means finding ways to compensate for them through the strengths in your staff. Hire people to balance your skills at work. For example, strong idea people with weak administrative skills hire strong administrators. Leaders high in entrepreneurial skills who procrastinate hire people who make sure ideas are executed. And if you are particularly strong-willed, fight your temptation to hire yes-men, and instead choose people who aren't afraid to speak up.

Finally, if you have taken all the practical steps to better the workplace but feel there are problems within yourself that need to be resolved, set aside time to think about and work on solving these inner conflicts, or consider getting outside help.

Admitting to a weakness does not mean you are incompetent in your job. It means you are realistic enough to surround yourself with people who will compensate for your shortcomings and that you are wise enough to search for the help that will give you the answers you need about yourself. What's more, by making these changes, you will create a more balanced work environment that gets the job done more effectively and harmoniously—not to mention the fact that you'll relieve the pressure that comes from trying to be perfect.

Be an example.

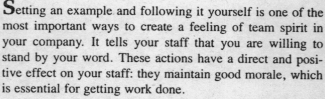

Setting an example and following it yourself is one of the most important ways to create a feeling of team spirit in your company. It tells your staff that you are willing to stand by your word. These actions have a direct and positive effect on your staff: they maintain good morale, which is essential for getting work done.

However, for your example to have lasting effect, make sure that you are consistent. If you want everyone to arrive by nine o'clock each morning, you must be there on time, too. If you want people to take a one-hour lunch, do the same. If you want them to follow good work habits—weekly reports, meeting deadlines, setting goals—maintain them yourself. By adhering to your own high standards, your workers will respect you more and probably will be more willing to join you in meeting your expectations for high performance and dedication. It is one of the most important ways to create a feeling of team spirit in your company.

If you drop into a careless attitude, it clearly can work against you. Resentment will set in because you've set a double standard—what you are willing to do and what you expect.

This week, note the discrepancies between what you say

and what you do. Write a list of these differences and work toward changing them. If you discover that you've behaved differently from what you expect from your staff, you may better understand why morale is low or your employees seem resentful. Begin to set a positive example. Once you do, you'll see how much more effective a manager you can be.

Communicate up.

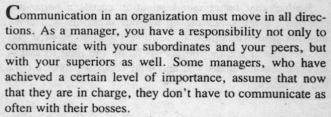

Communication in an organization must move in all directions. As a manager, you have a responsibility not only to communicate with your subordinates and your peers, but with your superiors as well. Some managers, who have achieved a certain level of importance, assume that now that they are in charge, they don't have to communicate as often with their bosses.

Nothing could be further from the truth. The lack of information only hurts you and the organization: it makes you look secretive and your company disorganized. It is essential that you acknowledge the importance of your role as it relates to your superiors. You need to communicate up to them. In essence, communicating up means that you are taking responsibility for what you do. You are keeping your boss informed so that he has no surprises, good or bad, and you are letting him know you are open to learning from him.

This week, examine how well you communicate up. Are you offering too little information? Are you learning from your boss about how to be a better manager? Should you be teaching *him* your new ideas? Do you need to inform him that you need a larger staff to perform more efficiently?

Now commit yourself to letting your boss know more about what you are doing and how it fits into the overall goals of the company. Suggest plans for the future, report on outstanding staff members, and if it is appropriate, even offer positive feedback about management techniques or suggest changes. Most important, let your boss understand what you need to get your job done. Remember, too, that communicating effectively does not mean endless meetings or reporting everything that goes on. A monthly or bi-monthly status report will keep communication open, as will monthly or weekly meetings.

Realize that better communication equals a better-run company. Communicating up to your superiors will demonstrate your willingness to be more effective at what you do, because it means you are spending the time to assess and reassess the goals you and your superiors have set for the company.

Criticism can help you grow.

No one likes to make mistakes, and no one wants to admit them. But worse than having to admit one's errors is having to accept criticism for them. It may be even more difficult to accept that criticism can be constructive to your growth as a manager and as a person. But the fact is that it can be very helpful. It allows you to develop humility and let go of the pride that insists you must always be right. It offers you the opportunity to know what your responsibility entails. It gives you the chance to change.

This week, work on accepting criticism and understanding the ways it can help you grow.

First, accept that criticism can come from any source at work, high or low. Most commonly, however, it will come from your boss. Let's say your boss calls you in and tells you that you haven't met your production goals for the quarter. Immediately you become defensive. You know there are any number of reasons for your failure. The suppliers didn't deliver, and the holidays stopped work for days. But mainly the problem is that you set unrealistic goals for yourself because you wanted to outdo your colleagues. So the criticism is, to an extent, justified. But instead of clamming up or jumping into a blind self-justification, explain the situation and admit in what ways you were wrong. Accept the criticism and move on to the next project.

Accepting criticism from colleagues or subordinates is much tougher. It requires even more honesty with yourself and more patience with the person who is offering advice. But since they may know you and your work habits better, their insights may be even more helpful.

This week, try to accept criticism gracefully. Usually, this means only *listening* to what someone else is saying and thinking carefully about it later. By so doing, you will open yourself to the possibility that you are willing to take responsibility for yourself and change your habits. It will foster your growth as a manager by showing you the areas in which you need improvement. Best of all, it will help you let go of the rigid perspective that you must always be right.

Give yourself
pleasure.

To perform well at work, you need to be a whole, integrated human being who is able to create balance and harmony in your personal and professional lives. Have you done something nice for yourself lately? You may be working so hard that you've forgotten about your balanced existence. You need to reestablish the harmony in your life. You need to do something for yourself that gives you pleasure.

There are many different ways of finding pleasure. They may range from going out for dinner with a friend after a rough day, spending more time with your family, or getting away on a weekend trip to paying more attention to your spiritual life. Ask yourself if there's something you've been meaning to do for yourself or a part of your life that you've been neglecting. Attend to it now.

This week, take an inventory of where and how you give yourself pleasure. It's a surefire way to discover whether you are generating any pleasure in your life right now. If you find you are not experiencing enough satisfaction, do something that will bring you pleasure—and think about how you can change things for the future.

Whatever you do, enjoy. You deserve it.

Open your heart to the pleasures of management.

In order to get your job done, you may rush through the day and get caught up in all the activity, constantly casting aside your feelings. In fact, you may believe that the only way for a "real" manager to survive at work is to remain detached and act only from your head. But in trying to make yourself invulnerable to your feelings, you block your ability to appreciate any of the variety and richness that being a manager can bring. This approach may lead you to become narrow-minded about your job and may stymie your sensitivity toward your staff. Worst of all, it can deny you one of your most important needs—to take pleasure in what you do. This week, challenge your beliefs and open your heart to the pleasures of management.

To begin, examine how you may have closed your heart to your work, and how it is affecting you. Think about the way you've reacted to difficult situations over the past few months. Did they foster an inner tightness? A rigidity? Now, when a challenge comes up this week, open your heart. Let's say you have a staff member who is very good and has creative ideas but is not always liked by his peers or by your bosses. He is accused of having an "attitude." Your open heart will keep you from accepting their blanket condemnation and jumping to unreasonable conclusions. It also keeps you from doubting your own good opinion of him. Most important, it gives you the sense of security to realize that before you make a decision about him, you must separate his personality from his productivity and review his skills objectively. Once you do, you'll be able to see how he contributes to the overall goals of the organization and assess his personality in relation to his job performance, rather than *in spite of* it. You'll take pleasure in having made the right decision, a compassionate decision that blends the best qualities of your *head* and your *heart*.

This week, feel life's flow. Make yourself vulnerable to its ups and downs. You'll find that it will bring a sense of lightness, sensitivity, and compassion to dealing with the complex and unnerving everyday issues in the workplace.

Give yourself credit
for taking risks.

As a manager, you are expected to take risks. You face them every day. And whether your risks turn out well or badly, you need to acknowlege your willingness to make these choices. This week, give yourself credit for taking risks.

Your first step is to understand the wide variety of risks you take. They may be large or small; they may involve a few individuals in your department or the movement of the entire company. You may sign a contract for a multimillion-dollar deal one day and let go of a failing account the next. You may have to confront a staff member who is demoralizing the department or say no to your superiors when they want you to act against your principles. You may have to effect changes when you are happy with the status quo. You may not even be sure you are making the right decision. Your risks may even cost you your job.

Now that you are aware of the breadth of risks you are expected to take, make a list of all the risks you actually took over the past week. You'll see exactly how many risks you deal with every day. Now think about the energy that went into actively encountering those risks, and you'll see that taking risks day in and day out is not easy.

Any action that requires a decision is a risk, and as a

manager, that means everything you do. In fact, one of the reasons you were made a manager was your willingness to take charge. This week, give yourself credit for your strength and courage. Give yourself credit for taking risks.

Be available.

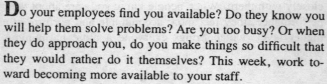

Do your employees find you available? Do they know you will help them solve problems? Are you too busy? Or when they do approach you, do you make things so difficult that they would rather do it themselves? This week, work toward becoming more available to your staff.

First, realize what being available actually means to your employees. It's an openness, an attitude. It's the difference between being just physically present and being actively aware of their needs. In return for your openness, you reap a multitude of rewards. You keep communication open, support initiative, and improve the work flow.

When you are unavailable, employees can feel isolated from the system in which they were told they were to have an active part. They may become resentful and even lose interest in doing a good job because they feel you don't care. If you don't care, why should they? For you, being unavailable keeps you out of control. As a result, you may find yourself putting out fires instead of keeping the office at an even keel. For example, if you assume your staff member is following your instructions on a project but don't monitor his work, he may be completing the work in a way that is totally different from what you have in mind. Not only will you be surprised at the results, both of you will be frustrated. You will have lost time and will have to do even more work. What's worse, your boss may also be displeased and will take his anger out on you.

Your availability to your employees can make the difference between a well-run operation and a splintered, unproductive workplace. You can create a positive environment simply by being available. This week, examine whether you are available. If you are not, make changes in your working habits. Establish weekly staff meetings, monthly lunches, or regular conversations with your people—anything to let them know you want to work closely with them. When people know you care about their performance, they feel more accountable and perform at a higher level, which brings everyone a more harmonious office.

Say what you mean.

□

How direct are you in your communications with your employees? You may often not say what you mean. There are many reasons for this lack of clarity, but two of the most common are that you are afraid of hurting your employees and don't want them to dislike you, and that you are unsure of your authority and need to put people down in order to feel better about yourself. Whatever the reason, the results are disastrous. Your indirectness clouds your messages and diminishes your power. It makes it difficult for your staff to know where you stand on an issue if you don't convey your intent through your words and your tone. You have to say what you mean. This week, examine how often you give a mixed message and how you can put an end to it.

To begin, let's examine what happens when you give a mixed message. The first thing you do is create confusion. Your statement is open to many interpretations. For instance, you may be inviting trouble if you say in a clipped voice, "Of course I like your work!" Or in a sarcastic voice, you snarl, "You think this is a good job?" Or with impatience in your voice, you say, "I really think you should do this job differently." The inconsistent messages have an effect on the people to whom you are speaking.

49

They won't know what you really want to say, so they won't know what to believe.

But if you give each of these messages in an appropriate tone, with a willingness to communicate what you mean, your results will be very different. If you say, "Of course I like your work" in a sincere and even tone, your employee will be more receptive to your questions and comments. But if you want to convey displeasure about how a job is performed, do so directly rather than with sarcasm in your voice. For example, you may want to say, "I like your work, but on this project you haven't delivered up to your usual standards." This communicates a positive outlook toward the person and comments only on the action itself. Your direct communication will inspire trust, and your staff will be more responsive to your requests.

This week, trust yourself to be open and candid. Make the connection between your words and your tone, and free yourself to communicate what you really mean.

Be innovative.

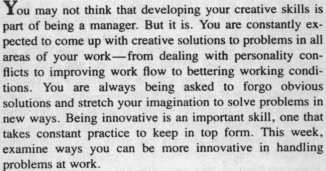

You may not think that developing your creative skills is part of being a manager. But it is. You are constantly expected to come up with creative solutions to problems in all areas of your work—from dealing with personality conflicts to improving work flow to bettering working conditions. You are always being asked to forgo obvious solutions and stretch your imagination to solve problems in new ways. Being innovative is an important skill, one that takes constant practice to keep in top form. This week, examine ways you can be more innovative in handling problems at work.

To begin, let's look at some examples of innovative problem solving. Over the past few years, companies and managers have become more flexible, more responsive to the way people live today. One of the biggest areas in which innovation is changing the workplace is in work schedules. With the prevalent use of computers, many employees can work from home, hooking up with the office computer system. Flexible hours keep certain departments (the print shop, for example) running on nontraditional schedules in order to service the rest of the company more successfully. Another innovative solution is job sharing. If two equally qualified people can work only part-time, the job can be shared. For working mothers, there are flexible hours, and an ever growing number of large companies offer full-time day care for children of employees. Some forward-thinking companies are also offering paternity leave in addition to the more traditional maternity leave.

These are examples of the breadth of solutions possible when managers and companies use innovation. Not every company will be able to offer such options, but your imagination, sense of adventure, and degree of caring about people's needs will help you to explore alternative solutions that you can implement at work. Even if top management will not allow you to be as creative and innovative as you would like, maybe they will allow you to put some of your plans into action.

This week, explore the needs of your department and your company, and examine whether you can bring change. Speak with your staff to determine what changes they might like. If any of these changes—in time, in working conditions, in duties—seems possible, plan for them. To convince your superiors, you will have to build a case for why these new systems can work. People are often reluctant to change, so it may take some effort to turn your ideas into action. But once you can convince them that innovation can get the job done more efficiently, you will be applauded—from all sides.

Remember, all companies want to think of themselves as innovative. It takes you to make it happen.

Let go of false responsibilities.

□

Stress, worry, and anger come with being a manager. Being a manager is serious business. But you can make your job even more difficult if you take responsibility for things that aren't really your concern. This week, learn to lighten up and let go of some of your burdens.

Begin by accepting the fact that everything that happens on the job is *not* your responsibility. You aren't responsible for your boss's bad mood, the messenger who delivered the project to the wrong address, the drop in the company's common stock, or acts of God. What you *are* responsible for are the projects you oversee in your department and your working relationships with your staff and your superiors. This is what lightening up and letting go will help you to understand.

Let's say you are in a politically difficult situation at work. You've just been put in charge of a major project. The problem is that your superior has not really let go of it. This puts you in a constant state of confusion over who's in charge and who can make the final decisions. But it's not your responsibility to second-guess your boss, only to do the job he asks you to do. You need to let go of some of the false responsibilities surrounding the project. Talk to your boss, clear the air, and establish your true responsibility.

Ethical issues at work may create even greater stress. Not only can they overburden your mind with responsibilities, they can affect your self-esteem. When you notice something going on that you disapprove of but say nothing, you disavow your true feelings, become resentful, and diminish your self-esteem. You're assuming a responsibility for silent complicity that you may not need to take. The next time the problem arises, let go of your false responsibility to accept everything you see going on around you. Speak up, voice your opinions, and lift your burden.

This week, examine how you are under stress because you carry the weight of taking on false responsibilities. Write a list of your duties and expectations for yourself at work and review it carefully. Distinguish your true responsibilities from your false ones. Then resolve to let go of some of the responsibilities that no one else expects of you. You'll develop a much more realistic and healthier view of yourself and your company.

Be fair.

Being fair at work requires a tough balancing act. It means hearing what people want, determining how you can fulfill their needs, and *still* getting the work done. Being fair isn't just a noble intention; it's a necessity. It keeps your staff from feeling frustrated (and potentially paralyzed) by "the system," and it earns you much needed credibility. This week, examine whether you are fair in your dealings with your staff and what you can do to improve your managerial style.

First, think about the people who work for you. Do you treat them fairly and consider their needs and goals at work? For example, did you redistribute the work when one of your three staff secretaries was swamped? When everyone in your department wanted the same vacation, did you set up a schedule that gave everyone some of the time he or she needed? Did you fight for someone's raise even when the company had a ceiling on increases? Your attitude of fairness will set the example and becomes the tone for how people will work with each other. When you deal equitably with people, your staff will be inclined to imitate your attitude and cooperate with everyone more freely. It also will allow them to view their workplace in a more favorable light and encourage them to be more productive.

This week, work at specific ways you can become more fair in your dealings with your staff. Pay attention to your workers' feelings. Talk with them and *listen*. Your staff will respond with the same goodwill.

Acknowledge good work.

Do you like to hear that you've done a good job? That your company appreciates your efforts? That you are an asset to your company? So why haven't you acknowledged your staff lately? Or told someone how important he is to the organization? This week, look for ways to acknowledge good work.

As a manager, it is easy to get caught up in your day-to-day management role and forget to acknowledge people. Or to find fault rather than give praise. But it is crucial for you to realize the many ways your acknowledgment of your staff can serve you. When you acknowledge someone for her good work, not only are you giving her credit for her good efforts, you also fulfill your job as a conscientious manager. You are letting her know that she has met your expectations of her and are encouraging her to keep up the high standards.

This week, examine your behavior and make concrete moves to acknowledge people when they are doing well. Be specific: note jobs that were completed on time or creative solutions to sticky problems. Then put your acknowledgments into action. Take your staff out for a leisurely meal at the end of a particularly difficult week. Let them stretch their lunch hours from time to time. Inform your boss of your staff's hard work. If someone's efforts were truly outstanding, write a memo for the personnel file. And if projects don't go exactly as you had hoped, acknowledge the positive aspects as you outline the difficulties.

Find ways to reinforce positive behavior by looking for and acknowledging good work. It is what you want for yourself and what everyone else wants, too. Most important, it will help to make you a more well-rounded, well-respected manager.

Delegate
responsibility.

☐

Do you find that you take on too much responsibility at work? In not delegating to others, have you become a slave to your work load? If the volume of work keeps you overloaded and overextended, and you do not delegate to your staff, you are being irresponsible. You need to know how to delegate.

When you don't delegate, you are unconsciously saying to your staff, "No one can do it as well as I can"; "They'll never be good enough"; "If I let go, things will fall apart." You also limit what your department can accomplish, because you simply can't carry an entire staff's duties on your back. If you delegate, however, you expand the possibilities for your department. You are telling your staff that you trust them to fulfill what you expect of them. Delegating also frees you to do what you are meant to do—manage people in their jobs.

This week, examine your work load and determine what specific jobs you are doing that you can delegate. Perhaps you are working on some projects that junior staff members could complete, while you simply direct them on the finer points. Maybe you need to realign your department and set up levels of management so you can have fewer people reporting to you directly. That will free you to direct your attentions to more important managerial or creative opportunities.

Remember, while you have a clear responsibility to know the overall goals of the department, you don't need to fulfill the goals yourself. Delegating responsibility forces you to set boundaries for yourself and for your staff —what you will handle and what you can train someone else to do. The result is more freedom for you and more efficiency for your department.

Let them get it off their chests.

A great deal of frustration builds up when people feel they cannot express their opinions at work. They harbor resentment, morale suffers, and productivity declines. This week, examine how you can help your staff voice their opinions and get their grievances off their chests.

First, observe your behavior with your staff. Do you close your door too often? Do you deliberately stay caught up in meetings and busywork so that no one can get close to you? Do you make coming to you so unpleasant that you are the last person they would come to with a problem? If so, your staff will hesitate to be open with you, and you will never get a clear idea of the morale and stability of your department. Ultimately, you open yourself to unwelcome surprises and "unexplained" turnovers.

These problems can easily be remedied if you set up a safe system for expressing opinions freely and without risk. You can provide these outlets in a number of ways, aimed either at the individual or the group. For instance, during personnel evaluations, you can encourage individuals to offer their comments. Encourage them to tell you about anything that is bothering them, and explain that you are especially open to suggestions about how they perceive you. To provide an outlet for the staff on an ongoing basis, keep your door open as often as you can to provide ready access. And if your staff members seem angry and frustrated, don't wait until they come to you—ask whether you can help.

This week, work on active ways to help your staff get their frustrations off their chests. You will alleviate frustration and build the trust that makes for effective teamwork.

Know what you need to be happy at work.

When someone asks you what you need to be happy, you usually think of your personal life: a happy family, financial security, a sense of meeting your spiritual needs. But what about work? You have the right to be happy in all aspects of your life—including your work life. Many people believe that this is impossible. This is a major misconception. You spend forty to fifty hours a week working, and you should like what you do. This week, think about what you need to be happy at work and how you can move toward achieving it.

First, take a self-inventory to develop a complete picture of your workplace. Ask yourself these questions:

- Am I happy with my job and my title?
- Am I being compensated fairly?
- Is my work challenging?
- Is my work environment pleasant and comfortable?
- Do I get along with my boss? with my peers? with my workers?
- If I could change some aspects of my job, what would they be?
- What is my ideal job?

Answer these questions thoroughly. If you come up with a lot of things you want to change, don't worry—all people want their jobs to be different from what they are in some ways. Now work toward making these changes happen.

Decide on two or three aspects of your job that you most want to change, and set a timetable for doing it. Be specific *and* realistic. For example, if you want to take on more responsibility, and the only way your boss will surrender it is if you come up with your own projects, start developing ideas. Set a deadline for presenting a proposal. If you want more money, build a case for it. Outline your accomplishments, have an idea of the increase you're looking for, prepare your presentation—and know how to counter your boss when she says no. It's also important to know what you will do if you find you *cannot* change your environment. In most cases, that means considering a change in jobs.

Ultimately, being unhappy in your job is a choice that you make happen. You have the freedom to change things, and once you have a clear idea of what you need to be happy at work, you can set your sights on attaining it.

Understand the child
in you.

When the alarm clock rings, do you find you sometimes want to stay wrapped up under the covers? Once you're in the office, do you find you have to push yourself to stay with the job, to take on extra duties, to maintain your positive outlook? What's going on? It may be that there is a battle taking place within you, between your adult self and your inner child. Usually the child and the adult in you can coexist, but lately, for some reason, your child is upsetting the balance. If this is the case, you probably are not meeting your inner child's real needs. Your inner child may want to relax and take life less seriously, but your adult self is overextended and under stress. Only by taking care of your inner child will your adult self be free to resume its responsibilities with enthusiasm.

One way to discover whether you've been neglecting your inner child is to take a close look at how you feel about work. If even getting out of bed for work is a chore, it may be that you don't like what you have to look forward to. Maybe you've overloaded your schedule and have been working every weekend for the past three months just to keep up. Maybe you haven't had a real vacation in years. Maybe you haven't even gone out to dinner or to a movie in weeks. The child in you is reminding you to create balance, so make some definite plans to nurture your child self this week. If you don't actively take care of the fun-loving, freewheeling spirit in you, she may make her needs known in ways that could be disruptive to your performance at work.

You also must know how to handle the more complicated issues that your inner child brings up. What do you do if your inner child simply wants you to be lazy because it wants someone to take care of it? What if the child is just being rebellious? In either case, you must listen to the child to find out what's going on within you. There may be deep-seated needs you have to address. This is when the adult in you has to step in—to simultaneously work with the inner child and pull its reins in so that it does not run your life.

Once you develop a realistic view of the inner dynamic between adult and child, you will be able to work out its needs and accept yourself fully. This week, challenge your inner child and bring a balance to your life. You'll be a more effective and understanding manager for it.

Have the courage of your convictions.

Having the courage of your convictions means being able to defend your beliefs whenever they are challenged. At work, this quality is essential but sometimes difficult to put into action, especially when the differing opinions are between you and your superiors. However, as a manager, it is your ultimate test: it is the most telling way you demonstrate your credibility as someone who can be counted on to be honest and trustworthy. This week, realize the strength that lies in defending your convictions and resolve to make this practice a matter of course at work.

The best way to integrate your convictions into your work is to find the most efficient and convincing way of presenting them to others. To do this, you must have perspective on the position you are defending. You must master both sides of the argument at hand—theirs and yours. For example, if you have to defend a certain job and the employee who does it, you need to understand why your bosses disapprove of the man and the position. You may learn that only one of your superiors objects, and from there, you can analyze whether that person is reasonable in his objections or is letting personal feelings get in the way. Next, closely examine yourself in the same way. Are you fighting the cause to satisfy your ego or because it is right for the organization? Be honest. Going through this process is the only way you can be clear about what you believe in and thus defend it completely.

This week, challenge yourself to know your convictions—and those of your opponents. Only then will you be able to stand by and support your beliefs for the right reasons.

Understand your organization's personality.

Organizations are comprised of people, and people have personalities. They transfer those personalities to their organization. In fact, most corporations are a direct reflection of the people who make up the top management team. As a manager, knowing a company's personality will help you understand how to approach upper management, how to respond to management decisions, and how to gain a clearer picture of your place in the corporation. This week, work on understanding the personalities of the people in your top management spots and how they reveal themselves in the organization's overall personality.

The easiest way to begin to assess your top management is to watch it at work. Observe how they come to decisions, make statements, render judgments. Your investigations will help you to discover whether they function primarily from their minds (through logic and reason) or from their hearts (through intuition and emotions). Their language gives you the clues you need for approaching them effectively.

For instance, if your chief executive officer is logical and rational and always answers your thoughts with "I think," you would not want to approach him with only impassioned pleas. He wants facts; he wants the case proven to him. If your CEO deals with emotions and always answers you with "I feel" or "My intuition tells me," approaching her logically will get you nowhere. She wants to see your intuition at work.

Next, assess yourself. What is your primary way of making decisions? Do you work from your heart or from your mind? How does this blend or conflict with those around you? Do you feel you fit in with the personality of your corporation?

Remember, there is no right type of personality in the workplace. Just as people differ, so do companies. But it is important to understand your company's particular blend of heart and mind, both so that you can work with it more effectively and so you can discover whether it is the right corporate personality for you.

I will not be a victim.

If your average day finds you bogged down in too much paperwork, unreasonable deadlines, disappointing subordinates, and company policy that fights you like a brick wall, you may think that you are being taken advantage of. You may feel like a victim. But the truth is there really are no victims in the workplace. You do have power and you don't have to accept what *they* do to you. You can make a difference. All you have to do is to take control of your environment. This week, stop being a victim and start taking control.

First, examine the variety of ways you can begin to take control. For example, you can make a difference in how people perceive you through as subtle a change as body language. The negative messages and lack of self-esteem you project through hunched shoulders, averted glances, and bowed head generate negative responses. Positive signs, such as good posture and looking people straight in the eye, exude a message of self-assurance that will yield a positive response.

Next, think about the power of the subliminal messages you may be sending to your staff. For example, imagine you are directing your employees to do an important project on a tight deadline. Deep down, you are afraid they

71

won't come through. You feed subtle messages to them and to yourself that the project will fail. They feel uncomfortable, pressured, and, as you expected, they falter. You say to yourself, "I knew it. They're unreliable." What you're actually saying is, "Poor me, I'm a victim of my uncooperative employees." If you change your approach and project your confidence in them, they will respond to your expectations and will turn in fine work. Expect things to go right, and chances are better that they will.

This week, stop giving other people control over your life. Instead, find a positive way to reinforce that you are in control. Say to yourself, "I will be in charge of my life. I will not be a victim." Recall this thought every time you feel you may let someone take unfair advantage of you. You may even want to repeat it several times during the week as a friendly reminder. Then sit back and enjoy being in control.

Be flexible.

☐

Has anyone told you lately that you are stubborn? Do you find that it creates problems at work? How many times a day do you say no to your employees? Do you insist that it must be your way or no way? Do you find your relationships at work are difficult? If so, perhaps it is time for you to become more flexible. This week, explore the various ways you can become more flexible in your outlook.

For a manager, flexibility is a willingness to admit that you may not have all the answers. It means that you truly will listen to and consider opinions that may differ from yours. It means that you are willing to learn to flow with the attitudes of the people you work with to develop workable solutions.

Let's look at how it can work. You have chosen one of your people to work on a special rush project. However, when you approach him, he says he is inundated with other work. You want your project done *now*. If you are rigid, you will insist that he rearrange his priorities for you. After all, aren't you the boss? Stop for a minute and understand what he has to do. You may find you have to be more flexible and either shift your priorities or find another employee for the job. Whatever you choose, your flexibility will allow for more creative solutions that will please both of you—and get the job done.

Now that you know how flexibility works, examine why you may not be as flexible as you could be. Ask yourself the following questions: How do I feel when I give an instruction that someone ignores? Do I tense up? Do I feel I have something to lose? People who are rigid are often afraid that something may be taken away from them. They create tight boundaries to protect what they feel to be important to them, believing that if they transfer responsibility to someone else, they abdicate their authority and risk losing their job. With these ideas in mind, think about the inner messages that govern you.

Finally, develop ways to change. The next time someone says no and you sense a tightness developing, take a deep breath and say to yourself, "I will be flexible." Repeat this statement as often as you need. From your new stance, you will be able to explore new options and come to solutions. You may not arrive at solutions by the paths you had originally planned for yourself, but you may find that your results are more effective.

Don't procrastinate.

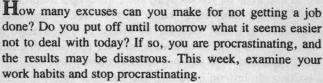

How many excuses can you make for not getting a job done? Do you put off until tomorrow what it seems easier not to deal with today? If so, you are procrastinating, and the results may be disastrous. This week, examine your work habits and stop procrastinating.

There may be any number of reasons why you procrastinate. You may not be ready to deal with the responsibility. You may not think you can solve the problem. The situation may be forcing you to face a limitation in yourself that you want to avoid. Whatever the reasons for procrastinating, the effects are wide-ranging, and most of them lead to trouble. When you put things off, frustration builds up, which causes you to procrastinate more. And because you haven't done what you expected to do, you become angry with yourself. This leads to more procrastination. Ultimately, you spend more time justifying your inactivity than completing what you had originally set out to do.

As a manager, your procrastination also has an effect on others. If you don't meet the schedules you set with your peers and supervisors, they will be as frustrated with your lack of performance as you are. They'll get tired of covering up for you, and you may even come to be known as unreliable. Your subordinates simply will find you impossible to work for.

This week, make a list of the things you've been meaning to do but haven't yet started. Examine each item critically. Are there any good reasons why you haven't worked on them? Are the projects too big for one person to handle? Can you understand the issues they involve? Are you just so overwhelmed with your work that this seems like one project too many?

Now break down your tasks into lists and set up timetables for completing them. Some of your projects may not be as important as you thought; you can set up a long-range schedule for completing them. Others can be delegated. Find the right staff member to handle it and arrange a meeting. The point is to review all your projects, big and small, and find ways to work on them one by one.

Concentrating on one thing at a time will free you from the burden of carrying too many unfulfilled responsibilities. You'll find it much easier to reestablish a working schedule that will set a good example for your employees. Best of all, you'll provide an immediate boost to your self-esteem.

Don't get bogged down in details.

Being a manager means juggling a lot of details. You are probably well acquainted with this fact. But do you accept it? You may tell yourself that you like being a manager, but all you really enjoy is dealing with the big picture—setting long-range goals, traveling on company business, developing new ideas. You hate the minutiae, the details, the routine. You think that writing personnel evaluations, going to staff meetings, and doing budget reviews do nothing more than keep you from the exciting parts of your job. The truth is that the way you handle details forms the foundation from which you can function as an effective manager. Once you learn to complete these routine activities without trauma, you free up more time to be creative. This week, work on taking charge of your work routine and become a more efficient manager.

First, determine what percentage of your job is routine. Be honest. Is it 10 percent? 20 percent? 50 percent? If you have a job in which routine should play a small part but seems to dominate, perhaps something is wrong. Examine how you are managing the details in your work life. Do you ignore them? Do you find them so oppressive that you don't want to face them? Remember that all aspects of your job are important to your success as a manager. With that idea in mind, aim at approaching the details in the same way you do your creative endeavors—with energy and a stake in doing a good job.

You may find it helpful to draw up a schedule for dealing with your routine detail work. Set aside a specific amount of time each day to do paperwork—maybe early in the morning or late in the afternoon. Whatever you choose, stick with your plan as closely as possible. Your day will evolve into a balance of the creative and the routine aspects of your job, and you will find that you can accomplish more than you had before—when you were spending so much time trying to avoid responsibilities.

This week, challenge your attitude about details and develop it into the foundation for effective management.

Encourage the truth.

Encouraging your staff to tell the truth is the only sensible stance for a manager to take. It serves you on both a psychological and practical level: it forms a foundation of trust between you and your staff, and it protects you from encountering too many unpleasant work-related surprises.

For example, an employee who is running behind on a tight schedule may be tempted to keep his tardiness from you, thinking he will catch up over the weekends. If you don't keep up with his progress, you won't know about his problems—that is, until you've missed the deadline. But before you place the burden of responsibility for being honest on your employees, consider the reasons why they might hesitate to tell you the truth. Quite possibly, they're afraid of how you will judge them. They know you strive for perfection, that you want things done a certain way. They think that when something goes wrong, you'll blame them, so the only way to protect themselves is to evade the truth.

To fight this defensiveness, actively encourage your workers to tell the truth. Remind them that if they try to cover up a problem or a mistake, it will probably reveal itself later, in more detrimental ways. Let them know how important it is to discuss concerns with you as soon as they arise. And when they come to you, be nonjudgmental and flexible. Listen to what they have to say; don't criticize them for having problems. If you don't like what they're telling you, don't overreact and jump into a rage. If someone is off schedule, find ways to work together to help him meet the deadlines. Even change the deadlines.

Finally, remember that the most important way you can encourage your workers to tell the truth is to be an example of that behavior yourself. Be willing to admit the faults and mistakes you've made at work; that will make it easier for them to do the same.

This week, encourage the truth. You'll build a workplace without surprises and an environment of trust.

Balance your leadership with their needs.

Do you ever notice how you have to treat each member of your staff differently to attain the same results? How the individuals vary in the way they respond to you? How, at times, your staff seem to be managing you as much as you're managing them? The fact is that as a manager, you will be constantly juggling your management style to fit your workers' needs. Just as you have a specific outlook as a manager, your staff members each have separate, individual needs. And the sooner you are able to uncover them, the sooner you will be able to develop effective management techniques that not only address their needs but fit in with your management style. This week, get to know your staff as individuals and determine what kind of leadership each person needs.

As a manager, you will find that there are two distinct types of employees: those who are self-motivated and need only your support and others who are less secure and need firm direction. Though each person may have a mix of styles, usually one predominates. For that reason, it may be a good starting point for you to consider these two types of leadership needs—supportive and directional—as the bases for your managerial styles.

With supportive leadership, you acknowledge that the

person you are managing is a creative leader who needs to be accepted in such a role. That means you cannot stifle your employee's motivation by trying to direct the person to follow a certain way of doing things. You need to give your employee more free rein; but in so doing, you must also support decisions to do things in ways that may differ from your original plans. A directional leadership style is for the person who clearly needs guidance, someone who is good with details, a hard worker, but not motivated to make an independent move. In this case, your clear goals and direction will help the employee get the job done— and provide the confidence that will encourage the person to make independent decisions in the future.

Finally, keep in mind that what your workers need from you may change. A self-motivated person who usually works on her own may need direction from time to time, and someone who usually needs direction may want to be left alone every so often.

Making the effort to develop adaptable managerial styles that are sensitive to individual workers' needs will create a more productive work setting, enabling your staff to work to their potential, and you to fulfill your goals as well.

Offer feedback regularly.

☐

As a manager, you know that setting goals is an important technique for ensuring that projects are completed, charting your company's growth, and maintaining employees' self-esteem. That's why you probably spend the beginning of every planning year setting goals with your staff and explaining the rationale behind them. But remember that the follow-up to this goal-setting is just as important—it's an essential part of the goal-setting process. It helps you to communicate your expectations and disappointments on a regular basis and demonstrates that you are actively involved in meeting the department's goals. This week, reassess how you help your people meet their goals, and sharpen your methods of offering them the feedback they need.

How do you offer feedback? Are you formal or informal? To be your best, you should offer feedback through a mix of styles. Keep up your formal ties to your staff, such as weekly staff meetings; they're simple but effective ways to chart the progress of departmental projects. Develop a new perspective on your company's yearly and biyearly employee reviews: they can provide a good opportunity to review past progress and chart the future; so take these reviews seriously and use them as concrete planning tools.

Next, think of the informal ways you can offer feedback. Observe your people regularly and stop in their office when they seem to be encountering problems. An early-morning chat over coffee can be as effective in building trust and offering feedback as a formal review. After-hours meetings are also good: everyone loosens up a bit. Perhaps some six-o'clock planning sessions could work up new ideas.

No matter what your mix of techniques, your main goal is to offer feedback as often as possible. Answer questions. Offer counsel. Tell your people what you think and why. It will show them that you are involved in their work and want to help them meet their goals. In return, your employees will keep their lines of communication open and thus provide you with a clearer sense of the short-term and long-range movement of your department.

Keep harmony within
and around you.

Have you ever noticed how one person's mood can affect
the entire staff? How one bad mood can bring everyone
else down, too? Or how a good mood can lift everyone's
spirits? Acknowledging the power of moods is particularly
important to you as a manager. That's because it is often
your mood that sets the tone for the entire office. Your
sense of inner harmony can have a tremendous effect on
your staff. It can mean the difference between a hectic,
disorderly office and a calm, harmonious one. This week,
develop your inner state of harmony and find ways to foster the same harmony in your staff.

To begin, acknowledge your responsibility for the morale of your department, and realize what that actually
means. It does not mean that you must always be in a good
mood, never show anger, never reveal your true feelings. It
just means that you are aware of the example you are constantly setting for your staff. It means that you know
enough about the power of the emotions you display to
monitor any dangerous outbursts before they disrupt your
staff. Building this inner balance within yourself is the first
step toward achieving it with your entire staff.

The next step is to create a balance in your physical
workplace. Examine the particulars of your work environ-

ment to pinpoint the specific causes of disharmony. Observe your workplace. Is it generally harmonious or hectic? If your job involves tight deadlines, last-minute changes, and working late, you know that there always will be some disharmony. But ask yourself whether it is more hectic than it needs to be. Are you running it at a faster pace because it adds a bit of excitement to your life? Think seriously about the toll it may be taking on you and your staff.

Now consider how you can foster a more relaxed attitude at your office. Imagine that you've got a deadline tomorrow for your boss. One day to do two days' work. You can't slow your work pace, but you can develop a different attitude toward it. Trust that there will be enough time and start working on your tasks calmly, one by one. You'll find that the frantic nature of the project will take on a new perspective.

In the course of any work week, you will find yourself and your staff in various stages of frenzy. Remaining calm and maintaining an inner harmony in these crises will promote an outer harmony in your staff that keeps morale steady. People will trust you because you are more willing to take charge of the situation and will use your confident stance as an example of what their own performance should reflect.

Balance your personal and professional lives.

Is your personal life as important to you as your professional life? Do you concentrate on building your career because it keeps you from making too many frightening personal commitments? Or do you create a social whirlwind to substitute for your disappointing job? Being able to balance your professional and personal lives is an essential ingredient for being a fulfilled individual *and* a more effective manager. This week, examine your attitude toward your professional and personal lives and develop ways to encourage a balance between the two.

To begin, realize that your professional and personal lives are two distinct, separate entities that also effect each other. Now do a self-inventory for both of them. Make a list of the kinds of fulfillment you gain from work. Then do the same for your personal life. Remember that your personal life includes not only your relationships with family, friends, and community, but your dreams and ideals as well.

Next, examine your findings, with an eye toward effecting change. If you seem to be depending primarily on your professional life to bring you fulfillment, find more time to explore your personal life. Delegate some work responsibilities, leave the office at a reasonable hour, and stop bringing work home. This will ease unnecessary work pressure and will free you to rediscover your personal life. But if your life centers only on planning your weekend schedules, plan ways to devote more time to work. Put an end to the abundance of personal phone calls, long lunch hours, and lack of concentration.

This week, reestablish the equilibrium between your personal and professional lives. Learn to understand your separate lives and devote your energies to them in the right way, so you can begin to develop a more meaningful sense of satisfaction and well-being.

Deal with performance, not personality.

Do you like everyone who works for you? Are there people in your department who rub you the wrong way? Do you find that you must tolerate more differences in personality in one setting than you ever bargained for? It may be an unpleasant discovery for you to realize that you don't really like some of the people you work with. That's one of the realities of the working world. But as a manager, you must also realize that your personality preferences cannot interfere with your professional decisions about your staff. You have to learn to deal with a worker's performance, not personality.

This week, become aware of how many different personalities work for you and how your judgment of them affects your evaluation of their on-the-job performance. Review each of your employees, with a critical eye toward differences in your personal and professional opinions of them. Does anyone's personality affect job performance? If not, ask yourself why you are concerned about liking everyone you work with. Accept the fact that it's not necessary. Your prime concern is their performance—meeting your goals, the company's goals, their own goals. If the performance meets the standards, personality issues are not relevant.

What may be standing in the way of separating performance from personality is your ego. You want to like this person because you think he is a reflection of you. He's part of your team. To make him fit your ideal, you may even want to change him. In most cases, this brings only frustration for both of you and a damaged sense of self-worth on his part, which may show itself in his weakened job performance. He may end up wondering why he should overextend himself to prove his talents when you already seem to disapprove of him. But if you stop focusing on creating a mirror image of yourself, you will be free to judge him by his performance and will more readily accept him as a valuable, if different, member of your team.

Of course, if someone's personality does affect morale, you may have to ask him to change his behavior. This will require another set of your most delicate skills. You have to let him know the effect he has on his colleagues and suggest ways he can change his behavior, without making a personal attack. You have to transcend your judgments and make the good of your department your only goal.

Whatever situation you have to face, your understanding of the differences between performance and personality will make it easier for you to relate to your staff as individuals, work with them as a team, and build a more harmonious workplace.

Challenge your workers to reach their potential.

Is your staff becoming complacent? Avoiding their responsibilities? As a manager, it is up to you to constantly challenge your workers to reach their potential. Developing and maintaining a motivated, energized team is a constant job, but it is the only way you can be sure of meeting your department's current goals and future plans. This week, work on developing techniques that challenge your workers to grow.

There are many reasons why employees do not work to their potential, and just as many ways you can challenge them. But all of them revolve around two basic points: Managers have to make employees feel that they have a stake in the business and a responsibility to it; and they have to maintain day-to-day interaction with their staff to let them know their manager cares about their performance.

What are some of the basic problems of motivation? One of the most common results from feeling overworked, underpaid, and underappreciated. Usually your employee is punctual, hardworking, and creative—but now he seems to have lost interest. What you need to do is regenerate his interest and commitment to his work. In most cases, a gentle push or a concerned talk will do the trick—some way to let him know how much you appreciate his talents and how much you are depending on him. Your employee has no problem accepting responsibility; he just needs to be acknowledged for it. After you've talked with him, make sure you follow it up regularly with informal talks and warm support.

Now imagine a vastly different problem—the employee who always wants you to make decisions for her. In a word, don't. Unlike her counterpart, she *needs* to learn her responsibilities. So the next time she comes to you for answers, ask her a question that will challenge her and force her to think. Show her that she must challenge herself to do the work. Put the responsibility into her lap. Follow up with her. Set deadlines and make sure that she keeps them. Make sure she keeps you informed.

This week, look for signs of laziness and avoidance in your staff and act on them. They may show up in subtle ways, and even good workers fall into the trap from time to time. That's why it's important to challenge your workers on a day-to-day basis, letting them know that reaching their potential is their responsibility—and your expectation for them. Ultimately, it will make your job as a manager easier, because it will lift the burden of getting the job done from your shoulders and place it on theirs, where it belongs.

Be a willing
negotiator.

As a manager, you are constantly involved in situations that require you to be a master negotiator, either for your staff or for yourself. The issues may range from asking for a raise to keeping a staff member your boss doesn't really like to adding to your staff when the budget is tight. How do you negotiate to get what you want? You have to become a *willing* negotiator. That means not only understanding what you want or need, but knowing what the other side wants as well. Knowing both sides of the story is the only way to know how to compromise effectively and reach a mutually satisfying solution—which is the goal of any successful negotiation. This week, search for ways to attain a balance in your negotiating approach.

First and foremost, understand the importance of listening. Realize that you usually will be negotiating on a one-to-one basis with someone who, like you, wants to have her ideas heard and accepted. Her beliefs may be as strong as yours, and she is willing to fight for them. This knowledge is your ace up the sleeve. Understand this idea *before* you begin to negotiate, and you'll be able to establish a relationship of cooperation when the negotiations actually take place.

Now, be the one to take the first step. Approach your

negotiating partner, offer your terms, and start listening. Show that you want to understand her position and work with her. Most likely, she will reciprocate and will attempt to understand your position and cooperate with you.

Don't forget to use the information she gives you as a negotiating tool. Analyze what she is saying and how she is saying it. Pick up on the hidden messages she is transmitting through her tone of voice and body language. They will give you clues on what is most important to her and what she is willing to give up, which will give you a good idea of how hard she is really going to fight. With all this information, you will be able to remain in control of the situation and yet work toward a mutually acceptable solution.

This week, remember that negotiating is not difficult. It just takes a willingness to listen, to do your homework, and to reach a mutual yes.

Set clear goals.

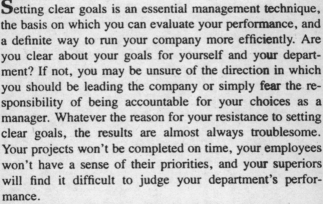

Setting clear goals is an essential management technique, the basis on which you can evaluate your performance, and a definite way to run your company more efficiently. Are you clear about your goals for yourself and your department? If not, you may be unsure of the direction in which you should be leading the company or simply fear the responsibility of being accountable for your choices as a manager. Whatever the reason for your resistance to setting clear goals, the results are almost always troublesome. Your projects won't be completed on time, your employees won't have a sense of their priorities, and your superiors will find it difficult to judge your department's performance.

This week, examine the goals for your department and your company, and make sure they are as clear as possible. If problems exist, try to pinpoint their sources. Have you been overzealous in what you expect to accomplish? Is your leadership wanting? Does your staff know what to expect from you? Are they not fulfilling these duties? Or are you just being unrealistic?

Now, work on setting your new goals. Be specific about what you want to accomplish and realistic about what you can expect. Set short-term and long-term goals, with concrete ways to measure your progress. A long-term calendar at work may be helpful with both team and individual plans, such as increasing sales by a certain percentage each quarter, having monthly staff meetings, finishing a project at a given time, and setting up individual meetings with employees each week.

Pledge to follow through with your calendar, constantly acknowledging the importance of what you've already accomplished and keeping future goals clearly in sight. If problems arise, ask why, then face them and continue on. Setting and keeping goals is never easy, but it will make your job as a manager more rewarding and more productive.

Be decisive.

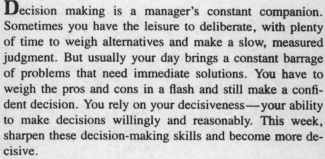

Decision making is a manager's constant companion. Sometimes you have the leisure to deliberate, with plenty of time to weigh alternatives and make a slow, measured judgment. But usually your day brings a constant barrage of problems that need immediate solutions. You have to weigh the pros and cons in a flash and still make a confident decision. You rely on your decisiveness — your ability to make decisions willingly and reasonably. This week, sharpen these decision-making skills and become more decisive.

First, examine your current level of decisiveness. How do you usually respond when someone needs a quick decision from you? Do you make one quickly or are you worried that you may make the wrong move? Fear of being wrong is the prime reason why people cannot bring themselves to make decisions. Your fear may be based upon a worry that your decision will cause people to dislike you or that you will no longer be seen as perfect.

To be decisive, you must trust your ability to make an evaluation and realize that you will not always be right. These two emotions go hand in hand: the more willing you are to take responsibility for being decisive, the more secure you will become in your abilities as a decision maker.

Learn to approach every problem as an opportunity to hone your skills. Remember that the more crises you face successfully, the more adept a problem solver you will become. And if, from time to time, you find that you've been wrong, don't despair. You won't lose your job, and your coworkers won't hate you; in fact, they probably won't even notice.

This week, be decisive. You'll lead a more efficient life, personally and professionally.

Count to ten.

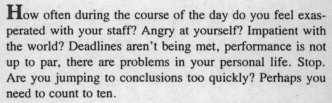

How often during the course of the day do you feel exasperated with your staff? Angry at yourself? Impatient with the world? Deadlines aren't being met, performance is not up to par, there are problems in your personal life. Stop. Are you jumping to conclusions too quickly? Perhaps you need to count to ten.

Basically, counting to ten just means waiting ten or fifteen seconds before you say a word. It's a method for slowing up and assessing what's going on around you. It's a way of pulling back when expressing your impatience may be counterproductive. More simply, it's a way of keeping yourself from overreacting.

How can counting to ten help when you *do* need to express anger? It can help you to focus. Let's say you've counted to ten and you still want to explode. You are angry, and you have a right to be angry. Your employee didn't meet his schedule and mouthed off to you. You have to show your anger. But now that you have counted to ten and let some time pass, you can express your displeasure more calmly and appropriately. You can focus on the event and not on the person.

This week, when a problem arises, count to ten. You'll find that you have a more positive attitude toward your

staff, a better understanding of what is going on, and a
tighter rein on your reactions. You may even develop more
patience.

Don't be complacent.

To live life to its fullest takes effort. It takes a willingness to say yes to life and what it brings. It also takes the determination to work for what is most important to you—whether it is how you perform at work, how you treat your family, or how you want to live. What stops you from attaining your dreams? In many cases, it is a sense of complacency—the passivity that makes you willing to settle for what life gives you rather than take the risks that will bring you a meaningful way of life. Complacency is a form of laziness, a message within you that says no to life. It works subtly and insidiously, gnawing at you from within. It is pervasive and controlling, and if you don't meet it head-on, it will conquer you. This week, notice how complacency affects your work habits and find ways to combat it.

Think about your job performance over the past few weeks. Examine how many times you've chosen to take the easy way out. For one, there have been projects and issues you've been meaning to take care of, but you never seem to find the time. As a result, you feel frustrated and angry at yourself. You feel that you're cheating yourself and your job in some way. Or let's say you are always batting around plans for revamping your department. But you never take any steps to turn your ideas into reality.

101

Why? You're afraid you'll fail; or you think that you can't fight city hall; or you think it will take too much effort and you're using all your energy now just to get by.

This week, instead of finding excuses, challenge yourself. Challenge the inner self that says no and teach it to say yes. Admit that you really want to say yes instead of no. You want to do your best. You don't want just to pass through this life; you want to make a contribution. Learning to say yes will take a commitment; it is the more difficult path. But know that by choosing yes, you are making a choice—a choice to give your best to life and live it to your fullest.

Now look at the specifics. What stops you from bringing change at work? What exactly do you have to do to break your cycle of inertia and negative thinking? How much change will it take? Whatever it is, you have to be willing to start on the path and follow it through. Begin with small steps and activities you know you can accomplish. Then move on to the real challenges.

Whatever you do, always give your best. Say yes instead of no. Don't judge yourself and don't worry about what others will think. Focus on the reward you will feel within when you attain one of your goals.

Consider work an adventure.

Adventure is finding excitement in what you do. It is seeing life as a series of opportunities rather than hurdles. Since you spend some forty to fifty hours a week at work, why not consider it an adventure and make it more fun? The problem is that for most people, working means exerting effort to get something done for someone else, with no personal reward. It's certainly not pleasurable, so words such as *fun*, *adventure*, and *enjoy* seem ridiculous. But if you challenge this belief and realize the possibilities, work *can* become an adventure, and a source of pleasure and self-fulfillment. This week, develop a positive attitude that allows you to see work as an adventure.

The most important way you can challenge your perceptions about work is to realize the potential of work you now think is mundane. For example, do you consider your work both boring in its lack of challenges and overwhelming in its duties? Do you grit your teeth as you walk into your office? Look at your situation from a different perspective. It is true that much of your job is probably routine; but if you can understand the opportunities for personal challenge, you may begin to view work as an adventure. A new boss may take some getting used to, but it may also bring a better rapport than what you had with your previous boss. A new client on the West Coast may seem to be an inconvenience, but it also may mean that you will finally have an opportunity to travel. A move to another floor may disrupt your day-to-day schedule for a while, but it also will offer room to grow and space for everyone in the department.

Considering work as an adventure is simply keeping an open attitude about life. It will help you to see the potential of a situation rather than its pitfalls. Try this new "open-door policy" this week and watch how your attitude—and your actions—are transformed.

Think of every day as Friday.

It's finally here—the last day of the week. You have two days off, and you look forward to being free from work. Thank God it's Friday!

Friday is a blissful state of mind. You feel a grand sense of release: your body relaxes, your mind clears. You feel you are leaving your troubles behind. You feel so good about life that you think you can accomplish anything.

If you are like most people, Fridays hold more of a sense of purpose and resolution than the other days of the week. You want to clean up the details from the week, so you work harder. You don't want anything to worry about over the weekend. You don't put off until tomorrow, because there really isn't a tomorrow—until Monday.

Now, think of how much more productive you would be if you thought of every day as Friday. It's not impossible—it just means bringing your sense of lightness and purpose to every day of the week. Once you do, you'll find that you'll start organizing your time better, will plan projects you can accomplish in one day, and will finally tie up some of the loose ends you have been ignoring. You won't put things off until tomorrow—because you have promised to get it done today.

This week, think of every day as Friday, and generate a new, freer rhythm for your life.

ABOUT THE AUTHOR

GLORIA LANZA-BAJO has a B.A. in psychology and an M.S. Ed. in counseling from Hunter College. As a national certified counselor, she currently conducts career guidance sessions with individuals seeking more satisfaction in their professions.

Ms. Lanza-Bajo has been an instructor at Marymount Manhattan College and has conducted career and management seminars throughout New York City.

Ms. Lanza-Bajo is vice president and division head of media and industry relations at the American Association of Advertising Agencies. Her expertise in the fields of business and psychotherapy qualifies her as both a career counselor and an authority on management techniques.